Food Zone

All About Grains

Vic Parker

QEB Publishing

Published in the United States by
QEB Publishing, Inc.
3 Wrigley, Suite A
Irvine, CA 92618

www.qeb-publishing.com

Library of Congress Cataloging-in-Publication Data

Parker, Victoria.
  All about grains / Vic Parker.
    p. cm. -- (QEB food zone)
  Includes index.
  ISBN 978-1-59566-772-4 (hardcover)
  1. Cereals as food--Juvenile literature. 2. Grain--
Juvenile literature. I. Title.
  TX393.P365 2010
  641.3'31--dc22
                                    2008056071

Printed and bound in China

Words in **bold** are explained
in the glossary on page 22.

Author Vic Parker
Consultant Angela Royston
Project Editor Eve Marleau
Designer Kim Hall
Illustrator Mike Byrne

Publisher Steve Evans
Creative Director Zeta Davies
Managing Editor Amanda Askew

Picture credits
(t=top, b=bottom, l=left, r=right, c=center,
fc=front cover)

Alamy 8t Keith Leighton

Corbis 19t Scott Sinklier

Dreamstime 19br Andy St John

Getty Images 19bl Stone/PBJ Pictures, 13b Dorling
Kindersley

Photolibrary 13t Age Fotostock/Frank Lukasseck

Shutterstock 4tl Tomo Jesenicnik, 4tc Jim Parkin, 4tr
PetrP, 4bl PetrP, 4br Anbk, 5 Alessio Ponti,
6l Jim Parkin, 6r Microgen, 6–7 Martine Oger,
7tl PetrP, 7tr Tomo Jesenicnik, 7cr PetrP,
7bl Fotohunter, 7br Anbk, 8bl V J Matthew,
8bc Gelpi, 8br Joe Gough, 9t Matka Wariatka,
9cl Russ Witherington, 9ccl Denise Kappa,
9cr Richard Griffin, 9cr Viktor1, 9bl Ukrphoto,
9br Fanfo, 10 Thomas M Perkins, 11l Robert Milek,
11r Konstantin Remizov, 12tl Anbk, 12cl Stanislav
Komogorov, 12bl Mosista Pambudi, 12r Mosista
Pambudi, 13c Digital Shuts, 14tl Tomo Jesenicnik,
14cl Bruce Works, 14bl Orientaly, 14r Alexander Briel
Perez, 15t Sarah Johnson, 15c Dusan Po, 15bl Ints
Vikmanis, 15br Rozaliya, 18tl Jim Parkin, 18cl David
Hughes, 18bl N. Mitchell, 18r Noam Armonn, 19c
Woudew, 21l Hallgerd, 21r Hallgerd

Contents

What are grains?

Grains are the fruits of cereal plants. More cereal plants are grown than any other type of crop.

There are many different kinds of grains, such as barley, oats, wheat, corn, and rice.

Wheat

Corn

Barley

Oats

Rice

4

Grow a... wheat plant

1 Put the wheat grains into your glass jar.

2 Pour enough water in the jar to cover the grains. Put the thin cloth over the jar and secure it with an elastic band.

3 Put the jar in a warm place. Rinse and drain the grains twice a day.

4 In just a few days, your grains will start to sprout.

Cereal plants grow from seeds. They shoot up as straight, tall grasses. Wheat is grown in more parts of the world than any other grain.

⇧ Grains grow at the top in clusters, or groups, called ears.

Where are grains grown?

Different types of grains are grown all over the world.

They need the right conditions in order to grow. Some cereals need lots of rain. Other cereals need the soil to be quite dry.

North America

South America

Corn plants grow well in warm weather and damp soil. The United States produces nearly half of the world's corn.

Quinoa (say *Keen-wah*) grows well in the mountains of Peru in South America.

Oat plants grow well in cool **climates** with damp soil. Russia grows a lot of oats.

Wheat plants grow well in mild, damp weather. A lot of wheat is grown in China.

Europe

Asia

Barley is grown in cool places, such as Eastern Europe.

Africa

Oceania

Sorghum is grown in hot, dry places, such as Africa.

Rice grows well in hot places that have lots of rain. Most of the world's rice is grown in Asia.

How do we eat grains?

We can eat grains at any time of the day.

For lunch, you might have couscous with red peppers.

For dinner, you could have rice with chicken curry.

In the morning, you might eat a breakfast cereal.

8

Make a...
wheatgerm smoothie

You will need

- 1.7 oz (50 g) wheatgerm
- 5 fl oz (150 ml) apple juice
- 2 bananas
- 18 oz (500 g) frozen berries
- Blender
- Glasses

1 Put all the ingredients in a blender.

2 Blend for two minutes.

3 Pour into glasses and serve.

Pastry

Cookie

Bread

Pasta

Doughnut

Pizza

We eat many foods made from flour, such as bread, pasta, pastry, and cookies. Flour usually comes from wheat, but other grains can be made into flour, too, such as rice and corn.

Why does your body need grains?

Grains are carbohydrates. **They give your body energy and should make up a third of all the food we eat.**

Corn and other grains contain **protein**, which your body needs to grow.

Bread made from wheat contains vitamin B, which your body needs to stay healthy.

Cereals such as oats and barley contain soluble **fiber**, which keeps your blood system healthy.

A grain is made up of three parts.

1 An outer layer called bran, which is fiber.

2 A larger part inside called the endosperm, which is mainly carbohydrate.

3 A small part inside called the germ, which is rich in protein.

Food news

Sometimes, just the endosperm in grain is used to make foods such as white bread. Other times, the whole grain is used to make foods such as brown bread.

Brown bread

White bread

How is rice grown?

Most rice farmers in Asia grow their seeds in patches of soil called seedbeds.

1 When the seeds sprout in the seedbeds in spring, the farmers replant them in bigger fields.

These fields are called paddies. They are naturally wet areas or are flooded with water. Rice needs plenty of water to grow.

2

3 The plants grow for three to five months. Then they are ready for **harvesting** in late fall.

Rice

12

4 Some farmers harvest their rice by cutting the plant stems. The stems are tied in bundles and left to dry.

The plant stems are beaten against bamboo to separate the grains. Other farmers use machines for harvesting.

5

You will need

- 3.5 oz (100 g) puffed rice cereal
- 3.5 oz (100 g) golden syrup
- 2 oz (60 g) plain chocolate
- 2.5 oz (75 g) butter
- Saucepan
- Greased baking pan
- Wooden spoon

Make a... puffed rice treat

1 Put the golden syrup, plain chocolate, and butter into the saucepan. Ask an adult to heat them until the chocolate has melted.

2 Take the saucepan off the stove and add the puffed rice cereal.

3 Stir well until all the cereal is coated in the mixture.

4 Pour the mixture into the greased tin and leave to cool. Put it in the fridge to harden.

Wheat

How is wheat grown?

Wheat needs plenty of rain to grow. Farmers sow wheat seeds in late fall.

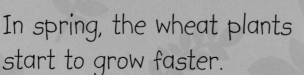

1 During winter, wheat plants grow slowly and look like a field of grass.

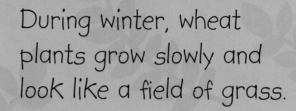

2 In spring, the wheat plants start to grow faster.

3 In summer, farmers use combine harvesters to pull the ears from the stems and separate the grains.

14

4 The grains are then turned into foods such as breakfast cereals and flour.

The wheat stalks die and dry out. This is called straw. It is then tidied into bundles.

5

6 The straw can be used for animal feed and bedding.

Food news

Wheat is grown in 42 out of 50 states in the United States.

Make bread

A lot of the flour that is made from wheat is turned into bread. Use this easy recipe to make your own bread.

You will need

- 4.5 oz (125 g) strong, plain wholemeal flour
- 3.5 oz (100 g) plain flour
- 1 tsp salt
- 1 tsp sugar
- 1 tbsp margarine
- 1 sachet easy blend dried yeast
- 5 fl oz (150 ml) warm water
- Mixing bowl
- Wooden spoon
- Greased baking tray
- Piece of greased or oiled cling wrap

1

Put the flour, sugar, salt, and margarine into a bowl and mix together.

2

Add the yeast and water and stir well. Use your hands to make the dough into a ball.

3 Push and stretch your dough for about 10 minutes until it feels soft and smooth. This is called kneading.

Put the dough onto the baking tray. Cover the tray with the greased cling wrap and put it in a warm place.

4

5

Ask an adult to set the oven to 450°F/230°C/Gas 8. Leave the dough for 30 minutes—it should double in size.

Remove the cling wrap and ask an adult to put the tray into the oven. Bake for 25 minutes until it is golden brown.

6

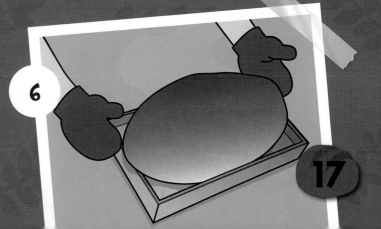

Corn

How is corn grown?

There are many different kinds of corn. Sweet corn is one variety.

1 Farmers sow sweet corn seeds in the spring.

Young shoots soon grow into tall stalks. The stalks develop ears, or cobs, of sweet corn.

2

3 Long, silky threads grow out of the sweet corn cobs, which eventually turn brown.

4 It takes about 2 ½ months for sweet corn to become ready for harvesting.

A machine called a combine harvester pulls the entire ears off the stems and separates the grains.

5

6 Some corn is taken to factories, where it is tinned or frozen. Ears of sweet corn are also sent to stores for sale.

Eat a... baby corn

You can eat baby sweet corn raw in a salad or add it to a vegetable stir-fry.

Make vegetable fried rice

Try using rice to make a healthy and tasty dish.

You will need

- 4 tbsp of rice
- 2 tbsp vegetable oil
- 1 red pepper, chopped
- 10 baby sweet corn
- 6 mushrooms, chopped
- Salt and pepper
- Saucepan
- Frying pan
- Colander
- Water

1

Put the rice in the colander. Wash the rice four times.

Ask an adult to put the rice in a saucepan and cover with water. Cook at a low heat for about ten minutes.

2

3 Ask an adult to help you fry the vegetables in a frying pan with a little oil for five minutes.

Add the cooked rice and salt and pepper to the frying pan. Stir and serve straight away.

4

Food news

There are more than 40,000 types of rice grown all over the world.

Basmati rice

Wild rice

Glossary

Carbohydrates
Foods that contain sugar and starch, which gives us energy.

Climate
The typical weather of a certain area.

Crop
A plant grown in large amounts to be eaten or used by people or animals.

Fiber
A part of plants that our body can't digest. As fiber moves through our body, it soaks up water and makes it easier for us to get rid of waste food.

Grains
The tiny, dry fruits of a cereal plant.

Harvest
To gather, or collect, crops from the field.

Muslin
A very fine cotton fabric.

Protein
A substance found in food that our body needs to grow and repair itself.

Notes for parents and teachers

- Choose a variety of food. Talk about which foods are made from grains, and which grains the foods contain.

- Use the Internet to research where different grains are grown and which conditions they need. Look at a map or globe to pick out the places where each grains is grown.

- Find photographs of what different grains look like when they are growing. Choose one for the children to draw and then label the different parts of the plant (roots, stem, branches, leaves, fruit). Talk about why our bodies need grains to stay healthy and how much we should eat every day.

- Discuss the difference between refined and whole grains and explain why whole grains are best for us. Make a picture list of how we might make whole grain choices instead of refined grains. For example, choose a brown bread sandwich instead of a white bread sandwich.

- Talk about how we might use different types of grain in cooking. Make an international grain cookbook, with recipes and pictures from around the world and recipes for the children to try.

Index